FOLK DANCES OF THE GREEKS

ORIGINS AND INSTRUCTIONS

BY

THEODORE AND ELFLEIDA PETRIDES

ILLUSTRATED

BAILEY BROTHERS & SWINFEN LTD
Folkestone

Published in Great Britain by Bailey Brothers & Swinfen Ltd.
1974

SBN 561 00202 9

Printed in Great Britain by
Whitstable Litho, Straker Brothers Ltd.

PREFACE

There is a great interest today in folk dances, not only those of the British Isles but folk dances of other countries as well. These dances have a particular quality about them which makes them free from the social frustrations encountered in ballroom dancing. It is a wonderful way to get "to know thy neighbour" and "let your hair down."

The dances of the Greeks are particularly interesting, for they have one additional feature which adds a distinctive touch to many of their dances: the leader of the chain performs intricate variations on the basic steps of the dance. This is similar to what you have in music when the soloist plays variations on the main theme spontaneously.

The reader may note apparent inconsistencies in the spellings of various descriptive words and names of dances; however, this was done to acquaint the reader with the different ways these words are spelled, as he is liable to find them elsewhere. Here are just a few examples.

Cyclic	Kyklic
Haniotiko	Chaniotiko
Hassapiko	Chassapiko
Horos	Choros
Karsilamas (Karshilamas)	Karşilamas
Naftiko (Navtiko)	Nautiko
Pidictos	Pēdēchtos
Tsamiko (Chamiko)	Çamiko
Zevgos	Zeugos
Zeybekiko	Zeïbekiko

Note: For all dances unless otherwise indicated—a step on one foot releases weight from the other foot. The foot without weight is held slightly off floor near former position.

5

If this book does no more than provoke comments, then it has achieved some portion of its aim, in that it aroused a lively interest in the study of the Greek folk dances and we can, therefore, anticipate further contributions in this field.

T. *and* E.P.

CONTENTS

INTRODUCTION

The most popular form of the Greek dance is the open circle with the regular handhold position; i.e., when facing the chain of dancers their arms resemble the letter *W*; hands are held out to sides, shoulder high with almost a right-angle bend at the elbow.

The next popular dance form is the straight line in which the outstretched arms are placed on the shoulders of the adjoining dancer. The straight line usually contains about five people while the open circle has many more. When the straight line contains many people, it frequently breaks up into smaller groups, as in the *Pentozalē*. However, you will find many *Hassapikos* danced in a circular chain, but, because the circle is so big, its particular touch, which is to mirror the steps of the leader, is lost.

Lastly, we come to the curved-line dance with its basket-weave hold. Every other dancer holds hands across the waist of the adjoining dancer. The left arm is over the right arm of the adjoined dancer.

There are, of course, various other formations and handholds plus variations of the above, but for our intents and purposes those mentioned will suffice; the type and amount of floor space available and the number of people on it will often determine the form of the chain.

When dancing the *Zeybekiko, Tsifte Telli* and *Karsilamas* as couple dances, the partners stand on the rim of an imaginary circle about five feet in diameter, facing each other. When starting out, the first few steps will be similar for each partner but as the dance progresses, they move independently of each other, vying for each other's attention. Occasionally, they will circle each other.

There are two basic categories of Greek dances, the *Syrto*

9

and the *Pēdēchto*. The syrto dances are those in which the feet move over the ground in a dragging or shuffling motion while the pēdēchto dances contain hopping, jumping, stamping, leaping or springing steps. There are some dances which contain both.

There are also basic variations in steps. In the mountainous regions, they tend to be slow pēdēchtos and a few slow syrtos; in flat land areas they are syrto and pēdēchto and the feet seem to pound the ground, while on the islands and coastal sections the syrtos have more of a lilt to them and the pēdēchtos are light with tricky footwork.

There are dances which historically go even further back, such as the hobby-horse dances performed during carnivals, and dances in which the performers don animal skins and masks; such as those of bears, goats and sheep; quite often bells are attached. Sometimes you hear the dancers hissing. This represents the hissing of large birds on the attack or even the snake. All the above were symbolisms of the Great Goddess and later Dyonēsios.

Quaint customs are also attached to the dances, especially wedding dances, which are too numerous to mention. These customs go back to mystical rites and the earliest of them related to the worship of mother earth, Graea, which name gives us the name of the country Graecia (Greece) meaning mainland; and the moon goddess, Selene, Helen, Hellen, Helle, from which we obtain the name of the people—Hellenes.

RECORDS

Two stereo records just released by EMIAL, Greece's leading record company, contain a wide variety of traditional and popular dance melodies that can be used with the dances described in this book. Both the records have been produced for international distribution and should be readily obtainable in this country under a Special EMI Columbia label.

Greece is . . . FOLKLORE (PSCXG 502) consists of fourteen dance melodies from the very varied folk music tradition. The rhythm and style, and also the kinds of instruments played, differs from one region to another. Side A includes island songs and songs from the northern mainland – Macedonia and Epirus – and also one song from Pontus. Side B is devoted to songs of the Peloponnesus, the southern part of Greece. The dance rhythms are those of the Syrtos, the Kalamatianos, the Tsamikos and the Serra dance of Pontus.

Greece is . . . DANCES (PSCXG 503) is a record of Greek 'popular' dances, which generally speaking are more stylized forms of many of the traditional folk dances. Here there is the Sirtaki, and the slow folk dance known as the Hasapikos from which it developed. There is also the Hasaposervikos, the fast form of the Hasapikos, which was originally the dance of the Guild of Butchers of Constantinople. There are also versions of the Zeimbekikos, the Karsilamas and the Tsiftedili (Tsifte Telli) – the provocative belly-dance famous throughout the Middle East as well as in Greece.

BALLOS

(Zeugos Choros)

The ballos, strictly speaking, is a couple dance. The Greeks have a few couple dances; however, the ballos refers to that particular type as is danced in the Greek islands of the Mediterranean; these dances usually have local names as well. When the Italians saw the Greeks dancing these couple dances, they called them "Ballo" which is the name of a popular form of medieval couple dance.

The music for the syrto (e.g. Selybriano) and the ballos are practically indistinguishable, indeed quite often the ballos is preceeded by a syrto.

We have, therefore, three basic types of ballos:

(1) Couples, when facing line of direction—men in inner circle, girls in outer circle—use regular handhold or hold left hands, other hand on hip, promenade position. Dance with opposite footwork, i.e., man starts on left and girl starts on right.

(2) Couples are first in an open circle chain with regular W handhold and dance a syrto before breaking up into separate couples. Here footwork will be the same.

(3) Couples are in an open circle chain, with regular W handhold. Only one couple at a time breaks from the circle and dances in the centre, while the others continue the syrto around them.

The music for this type of syrto and the ballos has a particular lilt to it which makes it easily distinguishable. Those of the coasts of Thrace and Karamania have an interesting feature; the singing of a lament (mánes or amánes), sousta politikē or ballos smyrneïkos. (The syrto tsifte telli is similar to Ballos #3 but the music is a little different—see Tsifte Telli.) The movement of the dancers represents the graceful gliding up and down of the caïques through the water.

13

The love motif is a mimic expression of mating birds (doves, pigeons, etc.). The outstretched arms (i.e., wings) herding the girls from one place to another and showing off (strutting) before them.

Characteristics:　Gay and lilting.
Formation:　Open circle moving counter-clockwise, usually regular W handhold, or same handhold shoulder high, promenade position.
Time:　2/4.
Steps:　Slow, quick, quick. (size: long, short, short.)

A

I—(*a*)　Running Step
　　　　For the man (opposite footwork for the woman)

　1 &　Forward l.
　2　　Forward r.
　&　　Forward l.

　1 &　Forward r.
　2　　Forward l.
　&　　Forward r.

　(*b*)　Running Balance Step

　1 &　Forward l.
　2　　Forward r.
　&　　Forward l.

　1 &　Backward r.
　2　　Backward l.
　&　　Backward r. next to l.

(When introduced from a syrto, both men and women when dancing as couples, use steps as mentioned above for the woman.)

II—Same as I except figure is performed backwards.

III—(a)   Running Step (obliquely)

   1 &   Forward r.
   2   Forward l.
   &   Forward r. up to l.

   1 &   Forward l.
   2   Forward r.
   &   Forward l. up to r.

(b)   Front Cross Balance

   1 &   Forward r.
   2   Forward l.
   &   Forward r. up to l.

      Turn ¼ to the left
   1 &   Forward l.
   2   Forward r.
   &   Forward l. up to r.

(The above is the syrto introduction.)

IV   (1)   Running Steps (a)—when dancing with partner, used to move in any direction.

   (2)   Step (1) above performed in place with stamps facing partner.

   (3)   Step (2) above—jump into squat on both feet (slow); straighten up (quick, quick).

B

I Forward Cross Balance—when facing partner.

(a)—1 & Side. l.
   2   Cross r. over l.
   &   Step back onto l.

(b)—1 & Side r.
   2   Cross l. over r.
   &   Step back onto r.

15

II Can be performed to the r. first, depending upon with which foot dance begins.

III Can be performed with leaps—steps 1 &—2 describing a wide arc in front of dancer, shoulder high.

C

Travelling Cross Rocks: The foot which begins the dance is in front of the other foot. The steps are very small on the balls of both feet. The leg of the foot that is without weight, has its knee slightly more flexed than the other.

I—To the Right. (When travelling to the l., the opposite foot-work is used.)

    (*a*)—1 & Cross l. over r.
        2 Side r.
        & Cross l. over r.

    (*b*)—1 & Side r.
        & Cross l. over r.
        & Side r.

II—To the Right

    (*a*)—1 & Side r.
        2 Cross l. behind r.
        & Side r.

    (*b*)—1 & Cross l. behind r.
        2 Side r.
        & Cross l. behind r.

Figures

I *Promenade* Step:
    Running Step: Couples side by side, Step AI.
                In syrto chain, Step AIII.

16

HANDS NOT HELD:

II *Turning and Crowding Step:*
Running Step AI. Man's arms out at sides, and the girl turns to right, keeping in front of his outstretched right arm.

III *Crowding Step:*
Moving in line of direction, the man moves backwards, step AII, with his left arm held across girl's midriff (not touching). The girls do Step AI. At the end of step, reverse line of direction doing same steps. The man's other hand is held out to side, fingers snap in rhythm. Girl's hands on hips.

IV *Face to Face:*
On last three steps of above figure, men back into inner circle and face partners. Girls face centre. Perform various figures, a few of which are given below.

V *Forward Balance Step:*
While girls do forward cross balance BI, boys will also do variation BIII or AIV(3). Boys keep hands on small of back for BIII and the arms are outstretched at shoulder level, fingers snapping when doing AIV(3). Girls can also do turns in place using running step variation AIV(2) with hands on hips.

VI *In and Out:*
Step AIV(1) is performed twice, passing right or left shoulders. Boys move from inner circle to outer circle and girls move from outer circle to inner circle. Step is then repeated backwards to return to original positions.

VII *Shoulder Flirtation:*
Running step balance AI(b). Boys in inner circle go out and in, passing girls first on right then on left. Girls in outer circle go in and out. Boys' hands on small of back, girls' hands on hips.

VIII   *Counter Circling Step:*

Step AIV(1) (dosey do). Two simple forward running steps and two simple backward running steps. Boys keep backs to centre of circle and girls keep backs toward outside of circle. Boys keep hands on small of back, and girls keep hands on hips as they circle around each other.

IX   *Circling Step:*

Do step CI or CII four times. Partners circle each other face to face after arriving at original position, perform AIV(1) to finish dance. Couples follow one another off the floor in either counter-clockwise or clockwise direction.

DODEKONESIOTIKO

Characteristics: Gay; with small, quick, gliding springs.
Formation: Open circle, moving counter-clockwise with regular W handhold.
Time: 2/4
Steps:

1   { (¾ of a count) Cross r. in front of l.
    { (¼ of a count) Step l. forward to l. oblique, weight on ball of l. f.

2   Bring r. up to, but behind, l. heel.

1   { (¾ of a count) Cross l. behind r.
    { (¼ of a count) Side r., weight on ball of r. f.

2   Bring l. up to, but behind, r. heel.

HASSAPIKO

This dance is one of the most popular forms of dance expressions to be found throughout the whole of the Near East, and like a number of others, has lost its Greek name and is popularly called by the Arabic-Turkish name for "butcher"—"Hassapiko."

Long before the Turkish conquest of the Byzantine empire, the dance was already popular throughout the area; it was popular during the Hellenic Age and was introduced by the soldiers of Alexander the Great's army. It was a war dance and was adopted from an ancient shepherd dance of the Macedonian-Thracian region.

The movements depicted a stealthy approach on the enemy; contact and battle with them; then victory. This was used to prepare the soldiers for battle; teaching them to move silently, signals for movements were transmitted by touch. As the battle ensued, commands were shouted and, in both cases, the shepherd, soldier or dancer was to move immediately into a new pattern. Finally the music speeded up so much that it was almost impossible to keep up with it—this depicted the victory.

It is this dance that the Butchers Guild of Constantinople adopted and was called during Byzantine days, Makellarion Horon. (*makellarios*: the Greek word for butcher).

This dance today has actually broken up into two distinct parts; there is no gradual acceleration and the very wild section at the end has been dropped altogether. There remains the slow Hassapiko *(Vari* or *Argho)* which is also known as the Naftiko (Sailor's dance), Ploioritikos (Stevedore's dance), Peiraeotiko (Piraeus is a seaport of Athens), etc. The fast Hassapiko is simply called hassapiko or sometimes Zoero (lively hassapiko). General terms are also applied to it such as: village dance, festival dance, wedding dance, etc. However, as was mentioned previously, we find this dance throughout the Near East under

19

various names and guises—in Arabic it is the *Debka;* Armenian, *Soorch Bar;* Ukrainian, *Arkhon;* Romanian, *Hora;* Jewish, *Hora;* Bulgarian, *Kasapsko Oro;* Yugoslav, *Kasapsko Kolo.*

Both the slow and fast parts have numerous variations, with the whole line participating in the execution of the intricate variations, which are performed spontaneously, as the leader signals them.

Characteristics: Gay and carefree. A high-spirited dance on balls of feet with many variations and fast, tricky steps.

Formation: Open circle. Hands on shoulders. General movement counter-clockwise.

Time: 2/4

Steps:

1 Step r. to r.
2 Step l. in front of r.
1 Step r. to r.
2 Hop on r. and kick l. in front of r. at the same time.
1 Step l. back next to r.
2 Hop on l. and kick r. in front of l. at the same time.

Variations

1 Step r. l. quickly to r.
2 Step r. l. quickly to r.
1 Step r. to r.
2 Hop on r. and kick l. in front of r.
1 Step l. back next to r.
2 Hop on l. and kick r. in front of l.

1 Hop on l. traveling to r.
2 Hop on l. traveling to r.
1 Step r. to r., step l. in front of r.
2 Step r. in place.
1 Step l. back next to r., step r. in front of l.
2 Step l. in place.

1 Spring on r. foot and swing l. f. out in front of r. at the same time.
2 Spring on l. foot and swing r. f. out in front of l. at the same time.
1 Step r.
2 Hop on r., crossing l. in front r. (make 2 short kicks)
1 Step l. back next to r.
2 Hop on l., crossing r. in front l. (make 2 short kicks)

1 Skip r. (backwards)
2 Skip l. (backwards)
1 Step r. slightly to right side, step l. in front of r.
2 Step in place r.
1 Step l. back next to r., step r. in front of l.
2 Step in place l.

1 Hop l.
2 Hop l.
1, 2 Step hop r. lifting l. leg behind r.
1, 2 Step hop l., lifting r. leg behind l.

This variation is performed by the leader only:

1 Skip r., step l.   ⎫ (These steps are taken forward into
2 Step r., l.   ⎬   the circle.)
                      ⎭
1 Step r.
2 (Reel steps) Hop r., step l. behind r.
1 (Reel steps) Hop l., step r. behind l.
2 (Reel steps) Hop r., step l. behind r.

Note: a skipping step to the right is performed as follows—hop left, step on right.

VARI HASSAPIKO

Characteristics: Slow, catlike steps with legs moving sharply and tensely. Body is bent slightly forward.

Formation: Chain dance, general movement is to the right, hands on shoulders, signals of impending steps are passed down the line by hand signals on the shoulders, therefore the line is not very long, usually about five men.

Time: 2/4

Steps:

1   Forward l.

2   Tap r. toe behind l.

1   Brush r. foot next to l. as you swing r. leg forward.

2   Hold leg out in front of you about shin height (leader may bring r. hand forward occasionally and brush r. foot sharply by sweeping hand across from l. to r.).

1, 2   Swing r. leg in an arc r. around and set it behind l. foot.

1   Step l. behind r. and pick up r. foot, crossing it in front of l. at the ankles sharply, at the same time.

2   Hold.

1   Step to right on r. foot.

2   Cross l. over r.

1   Step slightly back on r. foot, lifting l. slightly off the floor.

2   Hold.

A change of weight step is frequently performed as part of the basic step, after the hold position step as follows:

1   Step on l., lifting r. behind slightly off ground.

2   Step back on r., lifting left slightly off ground in front.

JUMP CROSS STEP

Steps:

1, 2	Jump feet apart.
1, 2	Jump, cross l. foot over r.
1	Slightly lift l. foot off the ground and stamp it, lifting r. off the ground behind l.
2	Tap r. toe on ground behind l.
1	Brush r. foot next to l. as you swing r. leg forward.
2	Hold r. foot thrust out in front, slightly off the ground—straight-legged.
1, 2	Circle r. behind l.
1, 2	Circle l. behind r., holding r. in front of l. ankle.
1	Side r.
2	Cross l. over r.
1, 2	Step back on r., hold l. in front of r. ankle.

FORWARD RUSH & SQUATS

Finish basic (left foot should be off the ground).

1	Step forward l. with a slight stamp.
2	Step forward r. with a slight stamp.
1, 2	Step forward l. with a slight stamp, going into a deep crouch and dragging behind, the r. foot up behind the l. foot.
1	Swing r. foot out right oblique, about shin high, rising from squat.
2	Swing r. foot down in front of, and touching, the l. ankle—going into squatting position.
1	Rise from position and swing out r. foot again to a right oblique position, shin high.
2	Swing r. leg around behind and touching ankle of l. foot, go down to a squatting position.
1	Rise up again, swinging l. leg out to a left oblique position, shin high.
2	Swing l. leg around behind r. ankle, touching it and slightly lifting r. foot off the ground while going into a semi-squat position.

1   Side r.
2   Cross over l.
1, 2 Step back onto r.

Steps:

The dance is usually started with one of several figures moving on each count, such as:

  I   Standing with feet slightly apart and swaying from side to side slowly. Each movement gets 2 counts.

 II   Side r.; together l.; side l.; together r.

III   Side r.; together l.; side r.; together l.; side l.; together r.; side r.; together l.; side l.; together r.; side l.; together r.; side r.; together l.; side l.; together r.

IV   Lift forefeet up and move them apart by turning on heels. Lift heels and move them apart by turning on toes. Lift heels and move them back together by turning on toes. Lift forefeet up and move them together by turning on heels.

  V   Move to right. Turn on heel of l. foot and toe of r. foot (feet form inverted V); turn on toe of l. foot and heel of r. foot. (feet form V); turn on heel of l. foot and toe of r. foot (feet form inverted V); turn on toe to l. foot and heel of r. (feet form V).
Move to left. Turn on heel of r. foot and toe of left foot; turn on toe of r. foot and heel of l. foot; turn on heel of r., foot and toe of l. foot; turn on toe of r. foot and heel of l. foot.

 VI   Move to right, keeping feet together; turn on heels, then on toes; as you pivot, bend knees. When feet are set down, straighten up slightly.

VII   Lift forefeet up and move them apart by turning on heels. Lift heels and move them apart by turning on toes.

Lift forefeet up and move them together by turning on heels.

Lift heels and move them back together by turning on toes.

These steps are performed immediately after basic; sometimes in place of basic, as they fit the music.

PROP KICK

Steps:

1, 2	Step forward l.; pointing r. behind slightly off the ground.
1, 2	Jump onto r. foot, almost kicking l. foot, swinging l. foot forward pointing toe out in front slightly off ground.
1, 2	Arch l. foot around behind r., slightly lifting r. off the ground in front of l. ankle.
1	Step r. to right.
2	Cross l. over r.
1, 2	Step back on r., lifting l. ankle high in front of r.

DOUBLE CROSS STEP

1	Cross l. over r.
2	Side r.
1	Cross l. over r.
2	Circle r. around to cross over l.
1	Cross r. over l.
2	Side l.
1	Cross r over l.
2	Circle l. around to cross over r. or prepare for next figure.

SINGLE CROSS STEP

1	Cross l. over r.
2	Circle r to cross l.
1	Cross r. over l.
2	Circle l. to cross r.

25

These cross steps can also be done backwards; i.e., free foot is crossed behind instead of in front.

BALANCE CLOSE

Complete basic; (weight is on r. foot).
1 Cross l. over r. slightly lifting r.
2 Step back onto r. lifting l.
1 Circle l. around behind r.
2 Slide r. next to l. (to close).

KARSILAMAS

(Antikristos)

This dance stems from an ancient Greek Pyrrhic dance, the vestiges of which were preserved by the Byzantines. The dance was popular on both sides of the Marmara around Constantinople. When the Turks conquered the area, the dance was adopted by them with modifications; it lost its warlike characteristics and gained those of a love-dance. In Constantinople where "social" dancing was confined mainly to women, the dance was performed for the most part in the home, and was called Panokato Horo, because of its counterbalancing, and up and down movement.

The dancers, generally speaking, move opposite to each other. As the dancers face each other, if one moves to the right the other does likewise; if one goes out, the other goes out; if one comes in, the other comes in. The same is done with circling movements, turns, etc. One is always counterbalancing the other. The term *Karsilamas* means face to face. Hence, the present-day Greek equivalent, *Antíkrēsto*. Although the predominant time signature for the dance is 9/8, other 4 and 3 accented rhythms are used. This dance is also performed in the islands off the west coast of Turkey and Cyprus.

As is the case with the Hassapiko, which developed in several forms, the same is true of the Karsilamas. The war-dances frequently began with a line-dance before the breakup of the dancers into pairs (or even soloists). This corresponded to the march or procession to the field of battle. (*Karsilamas* also means a processional.) The dancers would either dance opposite another group which moved to a similar position on the dance field facing them, or each performer in the line would pair off against another. The dance usually began slowly and built to a fast-moving climax.

For the most part, the dance became divided between two forms. In Anatolia the couple-pattern predominated, while in the Balkans the line was maintained. Here again we find a further division. In Anatolia, the love-motif set in and prevailed. In the Balkans, the line dance, when performed slowly, is a wedding dance; however, the quick character of it has also been maintained with it and is danced with quick steps, hops and a springy motion.

Characteristics: This dance is a couple dance. Like many others, it has lost its warlike characteristics and gained that of a love-motif. In olden times the Greek girls mimicked their Moslem sisters, holding a handkerchief by its diagonal corners, across their faces, so that only the eyes would show. They would tease their partners by moving the handkerchief by its ends, from side to side like a see-saw, and occasionally twirling the handkerchief in one direction so that its lower end would curl up and then quickly unfurling it by twirling it in the other direction. Finally her partner can't take it any longer and snatches the handkerchief away from her, and they continue to dance more vigorously and poetically.

Formation: Dancers dance opposite each other. Hands are held in an upright position about eye level, moving gracefully, or fingers may be snapped to the beat of the music. Hip sway is also used, single or double time.

Time: 9/8

Steps: Quick, Quick, Quick, Slow

27

1, 2	Side r.
3, 4	Cross l. behind r.
5, 6	Side r.
7, 8, 9	Cross l. in front of r. with pointed toe.

1, 2	Side l.
3, 4	Cross r. behind l.
5, 6	Side l.
7, 8, 9	Cross r. in front of l. with pointed toe.

1. Dancers move side to side facing each other, but in opposite directions.
2. Dancers flirt with each other over shoulders.
3. Dancers circle around each other.
4. Dancers move away from each other and then towards each other.
5. While girl does turns or circles around an imaginary centre in time to music, the man goes into a squat—either slowly, keeping his knees together and swaying with his knees from r. to l. until down, or he can go down quickly and, once in squat position, he can bounce on his toes from side to side, move forward, or do spins, keeping his arms up and snapping his fingers to the rhythm. Coming up is done in the same manner as going down, though it is usually faster.

Variation

Steps:

Quick:	1, 2	Side r.
Quick:	3, 4	Cross l. behind r.
Quick:	5, 6	Side r.
Slow:	7, 8, 9	Cross l. over r.

Quick:	1, 2	Side r.
Quick:	3, 4	Cross l. behind r.
Quick:	5, 6	Side r.
Slow:	7, 8, 9	Cross l. in front of r. with pointed toe.

Quick:	1, 2	Side l.
Quick:	3, 4	Cross r. behind l.
Quick:	5, 6	Side l.
Slow:	7, 8, 9	Cross r in front of l. with pointed toe.

Note: The above 12 steps can also be used in a Syrto chain (see Ballos type 3), while couples take turns dancing in centre using the 8-step figures.

Steps #2:

Quick:	1, 2	Forward r.
Quick:	3, 4	Forward l.
Quick:	5, 6	Forward r.
Slow:	7, 8, 9	Hop on r. (2 counts) hop again (1 count).

Quick:	1, 2	Backward l.
Quick:	3, 4	Backward r.
Quick:	5, 6	Backward l.
Slow:	7, 8, 9	Hop on l. (2 counts) hop again (1 count).

KASTRINOS PEDEKTOS

(Also known as Hērakliotikos or Malevyziotikos)

Characteristics: Dance is sometimes performed slowly and lazily, such as in Kastrines Kondylies or more quickly and animatedly with the leader doing various leaping steps.

Formation: Open circle or line moving forward and backward. Regular W handhold position.

Time: 2/4

Steps:

1 Step forward on r., obliquely right.
2 Cross l. in front of r., then shift weight back on r.
1 Step forward on l., obliquely left.
2 Cross r. in front of l., then shift weight back on l.

1 Step forward on r., obliquely right.
2 Hop on r., carrying left leg up and slightly crossed behind r.

1 Step back on l., obliquely left.
2 Cross r. behind l. and shift weight forward on l.
1 Step back on r., obliquely right.
2 Cross l. behind r. and shift weight forward on r.
1 Step back on l., obliquely left.
2 Hop on l., carrying r. leg up and slightly crossed in front of l.

Note: Cretan distichs (Mantinades) are sung while dancing Kondylies.

KALAMATIANO

This dance is one of the most popular dances in Greece. Originally a Syrto (full name—Kalamatiano Syrto Horo), it slowly gained the spirit and form of a Pēdēchto, so that not only the leader leaps and whirls in various embellishing figures, but the line of dancers will hop and skip as well.

This dance, as its name indicates, originated and was most popular in Kalamata, a town located on the southwestern shore of the Peloponessus; however, there seems to be quite a close connection with the ancient chain-dance called Ormos.

The rhythm of the Kalamatiano is 7/8, which in itself sets it apart from the Syrto dances, because, generally speaking, they are in 2/4 time.

The time of the dance is broken down as follows:
3/8 + 2/8 + 2/8 = 7/8   which again makes it different from other dances of 7/8 time.

Characteristics: Gay and carefree.
Formation: Open circle, moving counter-clockwise with regular W handhold.
Time: 7/8
Steps: Slow, Quick, Quick

1, 2, 3 Side r.
1, 2 Cross l. behind r.
1, 2 Side r.
1, 2, 3 Cross l. in front of r.
1, 2 Side r.
1, 2 Cross l. behind r.
Complete with Balance: II

Rare Variation

1, 2, 3 Side r.
1, 2 Cross l. in front of r.
1, 2 Side r.
1, 2, 3 Cross l. behind r.
1, 2 Side r.
1, 2 Cross l. in front of r.
Complete with Balance: III

Most Popular

1, 2, 3 Side r.
1, 2 Cross l. behind r.
1, 2 Side r.
1, 2, 3 Cross l. in front of r.
1, 2 Side r.
1, 2 Cross l. in front of r.

The line may use any one of the following balances to complete the steps of the dance as given above; i.e., the first half comprises movement to the right, the second half, the balance. The balances are listed in order of their popularity.

BALANCE I

1, 2, 3 Side r.
1, 2 Cross l. in front of r., weight off r.
1, 2 Weight back on r.

1, 2, 3	Step back l.
1, 2	Step back r., weight off l.
1, 2	Weight on l.

BALANCE II

1, 2, 3	Side r.
1, 2	Cross l. in front of r., weight off r.
1, 2	Weight back on r.
1, 2, 3	Side l.
1, 2	Cross r. in front of l., weight off l.
1, 2	Weight back on l.

BALANCE III

1, 2, 3	Side r.
1, 2	Cross l. behind r., weight off r.
1, 2	Weight on r.
1, 2, 3	Side l.
1, 2	Cross r. behind l., weight off l.
1, 2	Weight on l.

LERIKO

This dance, as its name indicates, is a popular dance from the island of Leros in the Dodekanese group. The dance is to the sousta as the slow hassapiko is to the fast hassapiko; i.e., a slow section which gradually accelerated to the fast section and which, in the course of time, became a separate dance unto itself.

Characteristics: Slow and heavy with a restrained vigour.

Formation: Open circle moving counter-clockwise with basket-weave handhold.

Time: 2/4

Steps:

1 Side r.
2 Cross l. behind r.
1 Side r.
2 Together l. or (*a*) slide l. to r., gradually lifting l. foot up
behind r. calf high, bending l. knee.
or (*b*) hobble onto r.

1 { (⅜ of a count) Step forward on l.
{ (¼ of a count) Together on ball of r. foot, knee bent.
2 Forward onto l.

Variation

1 Side r.
2 Cross l. behind r.
1 Side r. and quickly bring the l. to the r. slightly off the ground.
2 Forward l., together r.

1 { (⅜ of a count) Forward l.
{ (¼ of a count) Together on ball of r. foot, knee bent.
2 Forward l.

Note: The hobble step is actually a slight hop started off with the aid of a little push on the ball of the other foot with knee bent and which is brought up to the other foot before pushing off on it.

PENTOZALES

The name of this dance means *pento* (five) *zalē* (step) jig, and is typical of tricky, fast-stepping island dances. This was also a war-dance but served to test the footwork and agility of the dancers. Frequently the dance breaks up into smaller groups and they perform somersaults while in line, the leader always elaborating on the basic steps and leaping through the air. As the dance draws to a close, the small groups once again take their places on the line.

This dance also seems to be related to those dances which resemble hopscotch—the latter, however, being solo dances over swords or a mark in flour, meal, etc. If one keeps in mind that the islanders furnished the sailors for ancient Greek and Byzantine navies, and light infantry troops or marines, then it is easy to understand the necessity for practicing fast and tricky footwork. Running from place to place on a rocking boat demands perfect footwork and timing.

Characteristics: Fast and springy on balls of feet. When danced more vigorously and with leaping steps, the dance is called Ortsas.

Formation: Open circle moving counter-clockwise with shoulder hold. Sometimes danced in place. (Regular W handhold is occasionally used.)

Time: 2/4

Steps:

1 Step on l.
2 Hop on l. and cross r. over l.
1 Spring onto r. to the right side, swinging l. across in front of r. at the same time.

2 Spring onto l. to the left side. Cross and step r. in front of l.　⎫
1 Throw weight back on l.　⎬ These are three little quick steps.
　　　　　　　　　　　　　　　　　⎭

2 Spring onto r. to the right side. Cross and step l. in front of r.　⎫
1 Throw weight back on r.　⎬ These are also three little quick steps.
　　　　　　　　　　　　　　　　　⎭
2 Leaving l. crossed in front of r., hop on r.

SERRA

The name stems from its origin of popularity which is a river of Pontus, called the Serra. Two men break from the circle and dance a "Mahera"—mock combat with swords—in the centre as the circle continues to dance around them. It is for this reason the dance is also a "Pyrrhiko" (war-dance). In the past the dance ended with wounding of the adversary and was sometimes used to settle a grudge. When performed properly, the dancer's feet move so quickly that they appear to skim across the ground.

Characteristics: A very wild and exhilarating dance, building up speed quickly. It calls for all the vitality the dancer can muster and is, therefore, quick to sap his strength, for the action is continuous. The hands and arms tremble when held above the head as a man will do when shaking fists in a show of strength before commiting an act of violence or when he is enraged. The weight of the body is predominantly on the heels when dancing upright, beating out a staccato of three rapid beats.

Formation: Open circle moving counter-clockwise. Hands clasped and held down at sides. As dance picks up speed, hands are raised to shoulder level and, shortly after, are raised above the head so that from shoulder to handclasp to shoulder of adjoining dancer, it would show the outline of an inverted V.

Time: 7/16
Steps:

   I   1,2,3,4   Side r.
         5,6,7   Step l. behind r.

  II 1,2,3,4   Side r., together l.
         5,6,7   Step in place r. with a very slight bend of r. knee,

35

lifting l. foot about ankle-high and slightly backward.

III   1,2,3,4   Side l. to the left, together r.
      5,6,7   Step in place l. with a very slight bend of l. knee, lifting r. foot about ankle-high and slightly backward.

IV   1,2,3,4   ⎫
      5,6,7   ⎬ Repeat Step #II.
           ⎭

V   1,2,3,4   Step l. forward, together r.
     5,6,7   Step in place l. with a very slight bend of l. knee, lifting r. foot about ankle-high and slightly backward.

Variation for Step #I

1,2,3,4   Straddle jump (i.e., with feet apart).
5,6,7   Jump, crossing l. behind r.

Variation

There is a gradual movement to the right; the dancers move in and then out.

1,2,3,4 ⎫
5,6,7 ⎬ Repeat Step V.

1,2,3,4 ⎫
5,6,7 ⎬ Repeat Step II taking r. forward.

1,2,3,4 ⎫
5,6,7 ⎬ Repeat Step V.

1,2,3,4 ⎫
5,6,7 ⎬ Repeat Step II taking r. backward.

1,2,3,4 ⎫
5,6,7 ⎬ Repeat Step V taking l. backward.

1,2,3,4 ⎫
5,6,7 ⎬ Repeat Step II taking r. backward.

For the mock combat, the dancers move about with small running steps; quick, quick, slow. The dancers generally move towards each other, clash and withdraw. The clashes consist of one or a series of strikes upon one another's swords. Because of the primitive nature, 'the dancer is free to many movements, circling each other, squats, leaps, turns, etc.

Variation Used in the Dance

At the end of Step V, the dancers turn to right, facing line of direction and crouching low (Indian-fashion) with hands held low, V handhold, about knee high; do a series of about three step-hops and on the last, turn left and do three more step-hops against the line of direction, etc.

To right

I   1,2,3,4   Step r.
         5,6,7   Small hop on r., raising l. foot about calf height.

II   1,2,3,4   Step l.
         5,6,7   Small hop on l., raising r. foot about calf height.

III   1,2,3,4 ⎱ Repeat I and pivot to left.
         5,6,7 ⎰

To left

IV   1,2,3,4 ⎱ Repeat II.
         5,6,7 ⎰

V   1,2,3,4 ⎱ Repeat I.
         5,6,7 ⎰

VI   1,2,3,4 ⎱ Repeat II and pivot to right.
         5,6,7 ⎰

To right

Repeat movement to right and turn towards center and finish with Step V the same step which started the series.

CRETIKE SOUSTA

This dance has its origins in an ancient war-dance. Vestiges of its pyrrhic elements remain, in that the line comes out onto the dance area as it came out onto the field of mock combat (as they also do in the Serra). Then after centering themselves on the field, partners face each other as the combatants did. The dancers move their arms up and down, like the wings of a big bird such as an eagle, in flight; this is similar to the movement of the shields and swords or spears up and down, away from the body, sort of daring your opponent to make a try against you, and a show of strength.

Now the combat begins, as the dancers move through intricate variations, moving from side to side, in and out looking for a weak spot; the dancers have no set pattern, the steps are improvised on the spot, until finally only one dancer is left, having defeated all the opposition by either wounding them or by sheer endurance. In the modern dance, of course, one couple remains, better yet, some poor unfortunate odd man, who in days of old, might have been the hero of the dance.

The present name for the dance is derived from the Italian word *susta*, which means spring. When the Italians saw the Cretans performing this dance they called it by its outstanding characteristic, which is the springy movement of the dancer.

Characteristic: Light, fast and springy. The warlike nature of this dance has been obliterated by the love-motif.

Formation: Open circle with regular *W* handhold. Circle moves slightly counter-clockwise, then movement is reversed, going clockwise. Couples are then formed by men turning to their left and women turning to their right. Man holds his partner's hands, facing her, stretches arms out at shoulder level, continues to dance, circling to the right, moving arms up and down in winglike movement. Then circle to left. Man's right hand releases girl's left and girl turns right under his left arm and then left. Partners lock right elbows and circle clockwise, then lock left elbows and circle counter-clockwise. Couples break away, man moves away from girl, while girl dances, holding her hands clenched on her hips. The man does same; however, as he approaches his partner she stretches out her hands toward him as if to take him by his hands and as he stretches out his hands towards her, she teasingly rejects him by quickly placing her hands back on her hips, and turns back to him. This figure may be repeated several times. When she does take his hands, they can turn under, back to back, and do numerous figures by holding right hands facing each other.

At this point we wish to bring out that the original line was led by a man in front and man at the end of line. When the couples were formed, it left an odd man. This man takes one of the girls away from her partner, which brings on a sort of confused situation, for now the new odd man does the same thing to somebody else. This part can be called the mixer, since change of partners takes place (the men stealing each other's girls). Couples drop off one by one until, at the end, there is only one couple remaining.

Time: 2/4

Steps: (Quick, Quick, Slow)

    I. Feet together, spring on balls of feet, shifting weight quickly from one to the other.

1   Slight spring onto ball of r. foot.

&   Slight spring onto ball of l. foot.

2   Slight spring onto ball of r. foot with slight sideward thrust of l. foot.

&   Hold.

    Repeat above, using opposite footwork to the left.

II.

1   Spring sideward onto ball of r. foot.

&   Cross l. in front of r. (weight on ball of foot.)

2   Shift weight back onto r.

&   Hold.

Repeat, using opposite footwork to the left.

III. (Slow, Slow)

1 &   Jump slightly to right on balls of feet, l. foot in front of r.

2 &   Jump slightly to left on balls of feet, r. foot in front of l.

IV. Rapid succession of short kicks, straight forward in place and slightly off the ground. (Two kicks per beat)

1   Forward r., forward l.

&   Forward r., forward l.

2   Forward r., forward l.

&   Forward r., hold.

Repeat, starting on the l. foot.

V. Step lifts

1   Forward r. in front of l.

&   Raise l. ankle to r. calf, lifting r. heel off the ground.

2   Forward l. in front of r.

&   Raise r. ankle to l. calf, lifting l. heel off the ground.

1   Backward r. in back of l.

&   Raise l. ankle to r. calf, lifting r. heel off the ground.

2   Backward l. in back of r.

&   Raise r. ankle to l. calf, lifting l. heel off the ground.

Note: Step I is basic step used throughout the dance to travel, in place, turn, etc. Variations are used as long and as often as one wishes and can be performed one after the other or by interjecting basic in between each figure.

THE DODEKANESIAN SOUSTAS

These dances also stem from an early Greek war dance differing, however, from the Cretan Sousta in that it stresses the unit as a whole; i.e., the fighting line. The dance demands close body contact with the adjacent man and (giving the best shield protection) stresses the kind of movement one would have in a short wind-up and throw of a javelin or slingshot, or overhand strike with a sword; then a retreat back into position. The movement is also symbolic of caïques setting out to sea, being swept back for a moment, but moving relentlessly forward through the waves. But of greater importance than the above was the conditioning this dance gave to men who served as sailors or marines and who had to work in unison on a rolling or pitching ship in order to raise or lower sails, swing booms, move cargo, and any one of the numerous tasks which involves teamwork. (See Pentozalē.)

Today women also do the dance and the close formation is maintained by the basket-weave hold. The leader on the right does variations on the steps and performs various spins, leaps and acrobatics, smacking the soles and heels of his feet with his hands.

IKARIOTIKO

Characteristics: Since this island is close to the Dodekanese group, this dance is similar to the Sousta of these islands. However, it starts off like a Hassapiko, passing through an intermediate form similar to the Leriko before going into the third section. The first and second sections are performed as introductions to the dance. It begins smoothly with even steps, picking up speed and then becomes fast and jiggy.

Formation: Open circle moving counter-clockwise with regular W handhold or shoulder hold.

Time: 2/4

Steps:

I.

1 Side r.
2 Cross l. behind r.
1 Side r.
2 Cross l. in front of r.
1 Side l.
2 Cross r. in front of l.

II.

1 Side r.
2 Cross l. behind r.
1 Side r., swinging l. across r.
2 Side l. and step r. quickly up to l.
1 Side l.
2 Hop on l., crossing r. in front of l.

III.

1 Side r.
2 Hop on r., carrying l. along next to it, and quickly step on l. just in back of r.
1 Side r., swinging l. across r.
2 Side l. and step r., quickly up to l.
1 Side l.
2 Hop on l., crossing r. in front of l.

KARPATHIKO

Characteristics: Gay and festive.
Formation: Open circle moving counter-clockwise with regular W handhold or shoulder arm-hold.
Time: 2/4
Steps:

1   Side r.
&   Hop on r., carrying l. foot, knee slightly bent, then step on l.
2   Side r.
&   Cross l. in front of r. and step back on r. or hop.
1   Side l.
&   Cross r. in front of l. and step back on l. or hop.

Repeat, continuing on second count, etc.

KASSIOTIKE SOUSTA

(Danced in the Dodekanese Islands of Kassos and Karpathos)

Characteristics: Gay, full of spirit, springy and fast.
Formation: Curved line, basket-weave hold, every other person holding hands at waist level. Left hand over, right hand under. General movement is counter-clockwise; however, dancers move diagonally forward to right and backward from center of circle. All steps are very small and on balls of feet.
Time: 2/4

43

Steps:

Going forward:
1   Step r. foot.
2   Hop on r. and carry l. leg at ankle height, swinging it forward crossing over r.
&   Step on l.
1 &   Step on r.
2   Step l.
&   Step r.
1 &   Step l.
2 &   Hop on l. touching r. toe on floor for support.

Going backward:
1 &   Step r.
2   Hop on r. and kick l. leg out then, swing backward behind r.
&   Step back on l.
1 &   Step on r.
2   Step l.
&   Step r.
1 &   Step l.
2 &   Hop on l. touching r. toe on floor for support.

RODITIOUN SOUSTA (A)

This is the basic Sousta from which most Dodekanese Soustas are derived.

Characteristics: Gay and jiggy.

Formation: Open circle, moving counter-clockwise with basket-weave handhold.

Time: 2/4

Steps:

1   Side r.
2   Slight hop on r. (or slight double bounce on r.), step l. behind r.

44

1 $\begin{cases} \text{(⅜ of a count.) Side r.} \\ \text{(⅛ of a count.) Together on ball of l. foot, knee bent.} \end{cases}$

2 Diagonally back on r. to right.

1 $\begin{cases} \text{(⅜ of a count.) Diagonally forward on l. to left.} \\ \text{(⅛ of a count.) Together on ball of r. foot, knee bent.} \end{cases}$

2 Forward on l.

RODITIOUN SOUSTA (B)

1 Side r.
2 Slight hop on r. (or slight double bounce on r.), step l. next to r.
1 Side r.
2 Step l. next to r., quickly lifting r. slightly off ground.
1 Side r.
2 Step l. next to r.

The Syrtos

SYRTO

The Syrto, as it stands today, is a development of the ancient dance. However, as today, there was not only one syrto but many, and there were variations of steps within each. Therefore, what we have today are the remnants of these dances. In certain areas some styles and steps have been retained while the more unpopular ones have been dropped. The dances were performed to melodies of varying lengths, therefore, the number

45

of steps varied as well. A rule of thumb to remember about Syrtos is that they are generally in 2/4 time. The term itself means two things:

(1) To draw or pull—which means that there is a leader who leads or pulls the chain of dancers after him.

(2) To drag or shuffle—which means that the basic steps of the dance are of a shuffling nature as they move over the ground.

Two of the simplest syrtos are the "Epirote," "Sta Dio," and the "Nēsiotiko."

The addition of balance figures greatly enhanced the Syrto as did the pauses in movement (c.g., Macedonian and Cretan).

Whatever significance the steps had at one time, it seems certain that they were at least bound to some religious ritual and probably closely connected with the seashore. It is the most popular form of dance in the islands and shores of Greek lands.

This is in opposition to the form found in the hilly or mountainous areas where the Pēdēkto style predominates and the flat land areas where you find compromise of the two and the steps have a little more of a stamp to them.

In islands, when the dancers are familiar with all the variations, the first three men perform the same steps as the leader, while the others do the basic.

Characteristics: Dance with an air of solemnity or gaiety, depending on the accompanying music.

Formation: Open circle moving counter-clockwise with regular W handhold.

Time: 2/4

Steps:

The first example given is for a very old pattern which has carried itself over to a dance, commonly called today Cifte Telli.

1 &   Step to the side on your r.
2   Cross l. over r.
&   Almost together on the r.
1 &   Step back to the left on l.
2 &   Almost together r.

The second example given is for a pattern practically as old as the first and still performed today, though it is not very popular. With the body held erect and facing the centre of the imaginary circle, and feet moving almost as in the basic Tsamikos (Çamiko) with toes facing almost invariably to the center.

1 & Step obliquely back on r.
2 Cross l. over r.
& Side r.
1 & Cross l. over r.
2 Side r.
& Cross l. over r.
1 & Side r.
2 & Cross l. over r. and point toe on ground and hold.
1 & Step back on l.
2 & Step back r. almost together with l.

The third example, a little more popular than the first two, yet again not so widespread: with body held obliquely right and stepping lightly as follows:

1 & Forward r.
2 Together l.
& Forward r.
1 & Forward l.
2 Together r.
& Forward l.
1 & Forward r.
2 Together l.
& Forward r.
1 & Forward l.
2 & Swing out r. leg, pointing toe diagonally back to the right, turning body towards center of circle.

The fourth and most popular example of the Syrto is as follows (same movement and body position as the third example):

47

1 & Forward r.
2 Together l.
& Forward r.
1 & Forward l.
2 Together r.
& Forward l.
  Facing centre of circle do balance step.
1 & Side r.
2 Cross l. over r., shifting weight.
& Shift weight back to r.
1 & Side l.
2 Cross r. over l., shifting weight.
& Shift weight back to l.

CRETIKO SYRTO

As is typical of many island Syrtos, the leader performs various hand-slaps on thighs, soles and heels, does numerous leaps, turns and acrobatic maneuvers while the line moves smoothly and evenly.

Here we have the half-moon figure inscribed on the ground taking us back to a moon-goddess symbolism. It has a refined vigor and spirit, and with it comes to mind all the splendors of the Aegean civilization, when Crete was a thalassocracy. The dance moves generally to the right, however in certain areas the dancers move back and forth; in some places the dance is heavy and slow, in others quite peppy; the basic figure remains the same.

Characteristics: Depending on the feeling of the music. The dancer moves vigorously with sharp, quick steps or very smoothly, almost daintily. Leader will move a little forwards sometimes, then back. Occasionally will hold line with other hand (r. hand).

Formation: Open circle moves counter-clockwise. Regular W handhold.

Time: 2/4

Steps:

1 2 Point left toe forward.
1 Circle left behind right and step.
2 Step side right foot.
1 2 Cross left in front of right. Body facing right oblique.
1 Side right foot.
2 Together left.
1 Cross right in front of left. Body facing left oblique.
2 Lift up on ball of right foot and hold l. foot, ankle high.
1 Step on left foot, behind r. foot.
2 Side right foot.
1 2 Cross left in front of right. Body facing center.
1 2 Together right.

Note:

The steps to the Cretiko Syrto have been applied to the music of the song, "Misirlou." This dance was performed to the strains of this music, "just for the fun of it," and it seems to have been picked up by folk-dance enthusiasts throughout the country.

Actually though, it does resemble an odalik dance; i.e., a harem dance, though hands or small fingers were not held, and there is a slight difference in the steps.

NESIOTIKO SYRTO

Characteristics: Joyous with lilting movement.
Formation: Open circle, moving counter-clockwise with regular W handhold.
Time: 2/4

Steps:

1 & Side r.
2   Cross l. behind r.
&   Side r.
1 & Cross l. behind r.
2   Bring r. back but not quite crossing behind l.
&   Cross l. in front of r.

STA DIO

(Pogonissios)

Characteristics: In northern Epirus, the dancers are more animated than those in the southern part where only the first two dancers leap, jump and hop while the rest of the line performs the basic step in a more or less solemn attitude.
Formation: Open circle, moving counter-clockwise with regular W handhold.
Time: 2/4
Steps: (Slow, Quick, Quick)

1 & Side r.
2   Cross l. behind r.
&   Side r.
1 & Cross l. in front of r.
2   Side r.
&   Cross l. in front of r.

STA TRIA

(Stis Treis)

Characteristics: Gay but heavy feeling.
Formation: Open circle, moving counter-clockwise with regular W handhold.
Time: 2/4
Steps:

1, 2 Side r., then almost together l.
1, 2 Side r., point l. toe in front r. *(Face counter-clockwise)*
1, 2 Side l. to left and point r. toe in front of l. *(Face clockwise)*

Variation

1, 2 Side r. almost together l.
1, 2 Side r., slightly pivot on it to the left and touching l. toe on ground near r.; l. heel is off ground and knee flexed. *(Face clockwise)*
1, 2 Slightly pivot on l. to the right, placing it entirely on the ground and touch r. toe on ground near it. R. heel is off ground and knee flexed. *(Face counter-clockwise)*

E TRATTA

(The Fishing Net)

Characteristics: This is danced by women in Megara only at Eastertime, with air of restrained joy with proud bearing.
Formation: Quarter-moon circle, moving counter-clockwise with basket-weave handhold.

51

Time: 2/4
Steps:

1 Side r.
2 Step l. in front of r.
1 Side r.
2 Point l. in front of r.
1 Step back on l. foot.
2 Point r. foot in front of l. *(Facing counter-clockwise)*

Variation

The Tratta is also a Nēsiotiko, which is more lively.

1 & Back r. oblique.
2   Cross l. behind r.
&   Side r.
1 & Cross l. in front of r.
2   Forward r. oblique
&   Step together l.

TIK

This dance is one of the most popular dances of Pontus (Lazistan). Its name in Turkish means upright or support (which is almost similar to the Greek word *s-toich-os* which has the same connotation.) Actually, there are a variety of Tiks, the basic pattern being the same.

Tik *ston topon* (in place)
Tik *ston gonaton* (on knees)
Tik *galenon* (gently)
Tik *langefton* (leaping)
Tik *tromachton* (shaking)
Tik *diplon* (double, the music doubles in speed)
Tik *machera* (sword or knife dance)

The Tik also illustrates a part of life on the Black Sea where the dance depicts the quick movement of fish through the water and the "tromachton," symbolizing the aimless flutterings of the fish after it's caught and pulled out of the water.

One of the outstanding features of the Pontus dances is the slow raising of arms from the down position to the straight up. This is not to mean though, that the regular armhold is not used for most of the dance.

Characteristics: At first the dancers move rigidly with heavy steps. They stand close to each other shoulder to shoulder with hands and arms held straight down at sides. As the dance progresses, the dancers move more freely, increasing the distance between each other and their arms are swung slowly straight up into the air.

Formation: Open circle, moving counter-clockwise with regular W handhold.

Time: 5/8

Steps:

Quick: 1, 2   Side r.
Slow: 3, 4, 5   Cross l. behind r.

Quick: 1, 2   Side r.
Slow: 3, 4, 5   Step together l.

Quick: 1, 2   Side l.
Slow: 3, 4, 5   Step together r.

Quick: 1, 2   Side r.
Slow: 3, 4, 5   Step together l.

Quick: 1, 2   Side l.
Slow: 3, 4, 5   Step together r.

Variation

A   { Quick: 1, 2   Side r.
     { Slow: 3, 4, 5   Cross l. behind r.

B   { Quick: 1, 2   Side r.
     { Slow: 3, 4, 5   Cross l. over r., step back on r.

C	Quick:	1, 2	Side l.
	Slow:	3, 4, 5	Cross r. over l., step back on l.

D	Quick:	1, 2	Side r.
	Slow:	3, 4, 5	Cross l. over r., step back on r.

	Quick:	1, 2	Forward l.
E	Slow:	3, 4, 5	Forward r. next to l., shift weight back on l.

For *B, C, D* and *E*, a step-hop, crossing one leg in the air, can be substituted.

TSAMIKO

The Tsamiko, as its name suggests, originated in and was the most popular dance of the area of Tsamidon. The name Tsamidon and Tsamouria (Turkish *Çamouria*) seem to be corruptions of the ancient locality which they now represent and in the past was called Camania. The Turkish name for a person of this area is "Çam." However, during the war of independence, it became the favourite dance of the *klephts* (mountain fighters), and it spread from Epirus through all of Greece and is particularly enjoyed in the Aetolo-Acarnania area. It is not only symbolic of the shepherd's climbing and leaping among the mountain crags and ledges, but goes further back into antiquity, for it is one of the many dances which were associated with the sacred crane *(geranos)*.

This dance is different from the general type of war dance, for quite often, especially in Epirus, the beat is slow; yet because of it, the excitement stirred up in the individual, especially the leader, is more deeply rooted than in the faster war dances. The peak of the dance exhorts the leader to perform outstanding gymnastic and acrobatic feats.

The timing of the dance is 3/4, broken down in this manner:

1, 2   3

2/4 + 1/4 — 3/4 or slow, quick.

Sometimes the beat is in 3/8 and occasionally 6/8.

Characteristics: Dignified and warlike, with the leader doing many jumping and leaping figures.

Formation: Open circle, moving counter-clockwise with the regular W handhold. Right foot crossed over left always before starting this dance.

Time: 3/4 or 3/8

Steps:

1, 2   Side r.
3   Cross l. in front of r.

1, 2   Side r.
3   Cross l. in front of r.

1, 2   Side r.
3   Cross l. in front of r.

1, 2   Side r.
3   Lift l. foot to calf of r. leg, hopping on r.

1, 2   Side l. (moving clockwise)
3   Cross r. in front of l

1, 2   Side l.
3   Cross r. in front of l., pointing toe, and hop on l.

The sixteen-step variation is the more correct form of the dance as it was introduced to the rest of Greece from Epirus. The last four steps have been eliminated in the other versions which come from central and southern Greece and which are the most popular in the United States.

Remember, r. foot always crossed over l. before starting the dance.

Steps:

1, 2 Side r.
3 Cross l. in front of r.

1, 2 Point r. foot forward right oblique.
3 Step r. back next to l.

1, 2 Point l. forward.
3 Cross l. in front of r.

1, 2 Side r.
3 Hop on r. foot, kicking l. foot up behind about knee high.

1, 2 Side l. to left.
3 Cross r. in front of l.

1, 2 Side l.
3 Kick r. foot across l. shin while hopping on l.

1, 2 Side r. to right.
3 Cross l. in front of r.

1, 2 Point r. to right side.
3 Cross r. foot over l. foot.

Variation

The following variations which are described here can be used for other dances which make use of jumping and leaping figures such as the Kalamatiano or Zeybekiko, etc.

Steps:

Slow: 1, 2 Side r.
Quick: 3 Cross l. behind r.
Slow: 1, 2 Spring into air by pushing off on l. foot and throwing the r. leg up into the air about eye level high. The r. leg is to be followed immediately by the l. leg.
Quick: 3 The sole of l. foot is slapped by r. hand. The assistance for height in this leap is given by the second man on the line who is holding leader's l. hand.

Quick:	1	Side r.
Quick:	2	Swing l. leg into air at eye level followed by r.
Quick:	3	Slap r. side of r. heel with palm of r. hand.

Quick:	1	Jump on both feet in a little crouch.
Quick:	2	Leap up, throwing right side of body up into the air at eye-level height, keeping both legs separated with the r. leg behind the l.
Quick:	3	Slap r. side of r. heel with the r. hand, then circle the hand around and slap sole of l. foot. The variation of the above, for the first quick step, jump into a full crouch and slap r. hand on the ground.

Quick:	1	Jump on both feet into a full crouch.
Quick:	2	Slap hand on ground.
Quick:	3	Jump up into the air, keeping feet and knees together, throwing feet up behind, then slap r. side of r. heel.

The variety embellishing steps are practically endless.

Variation

Steps:
1. In balance, at the end of movement to right when kicking behind with l. leg, slap r. side l. heel with palm of r. hand.
2. In balance, instead of kicking l. leg behind r., cross it in front of r.—also palm slap may be done forward striking the sole of l. shoe.
3. In right balance, instead of kicking l. leg do two tiny quick steps to right by stepping on l., then r. carrying weight mostly on r. foot. (In the same manner for balance to l. but opposite feet.)
4. In balance, fake forward kick ending in kick behind leg.
5. In balance, lock free ankle behind knee and do slight knee-bend, arching your back backwards.

6. In basic movement to right, step r., l., r. together; l., r., l. together; step r., step l., then step r. and balance l. rhythmically as follows: S-Q-Q, S-Q-Q, S-Q, etc.

TSIFTE TELLI*

(Kelikos Horos)

The dance is performed either by couples or singly. The name means two strings which is in fact the trademark of the dance. One of the stringed instruments, usually the *ud* (a deep pot-bellied lute) or a guitar, etc., is plucked on only two strings when introducing or accenting the rhythm. The drum (usually a finger drum of an hour-glass shape) also accents two heavy beats: one in the centre of the skin, the other closer to the rim. The lyra (the great-grandfather of the violin) or a violin, etc., is frequently played on two strings. In the Near East this is usually done in imitation of a wind instrument such as a bagpipe; the bowed instrument plays a wailing melody.

There are several different types of Tsifte Tellis. The medium slow; the one with heavy, even beats which is closer to the Arabic; another is more melodious and sounds like a rhumba. There are two more, one of which sounds like a heavy Ballos and the other a light Ballos. The one that sounds like a rhumba is sometimes called Syrto Tsifte Telli to describe its movement.

The origin of this dance appears to be closely connected with the worship of both Mother Earth and the Moon Goddess. At one time there were specific movements which were identified with each dance, but early in ancient times when the roles of the goddesses became confused and the role of one was superim-

---

* The above is the Greek spelling of the Turkish name for the dance, Çifte Telli. The comparative English spelling would be Chifte Telli, the ch pronounced as in the word church.

posed on the other, the dance became a potpourri of different dance movements.

The undulating movement of the body and arms depicted both the movement of snakes, in particular Ophion (in the creation myth with Mother Earth), and water, which was closely associated with the Moon Goddess, Aphrodite. The swaying body often illustrates the swaying tree, while the flowing handkerchief is a visible symbol of the wind. On occasion an undulating or rolling movement of the abdomen was used to put emphasis on the "World Egg" which was laid; and you can easily see that this was one of the dances performed at love or fertility rites; today a dance containing this movement is called a belly dance; the ancient Greek name of which was *kolia*. The abdominal movement is supposed to increase the muscle tone of the intestinal tract and womb.

This dance was not only danced as a solo by a temple priestess or groups of priestesses, but at times the priestesses were also accompanied by men and, notwithstanding what was mentioned above, the general aspect of the dancer was that of a bird—usually a swan. The swan was one of the birds which was sacred to Aphrodite or whatever name she had as moon goddess, the man also playing the role of a swan slowly becoming an eagle (Zeus' symbolic bird) until he captures his partner.

The movements of the head and neck, shaking of the shoulders and the quivering of the hips are all movements to be seen in the actions of birds (watch water birds shake water off their bodies). The swan is also known to issue forth two trumpet-like notes while in flight.

The Tsifte Telli is one of the most beautiful dances in the world and yet the steps are simple. It was and is most popular in the Eastern Mediterranean where the worship of a moon goddess remained strongest; Western Asia Minor, Syria, Phoenicia, Egypt; and besides Aphrodite would include, under one guise or another—Ashtaroth, Astarte, Ishtar and Isis. In Ionia, the dance finally degenerated to such an extent that many lascivious motions and attitudes became a part of the performance and it was these actions to which the Romans referred as

Ionic movements. These movements were also found in their dances to Dyonisus.

Since the dance stems from the eastern Aegean area, it naturally contains elements of the Nēsiotiko Syrto and the outstanding and characteristic step in this dance was the arch, which was inscribed, on the ground or in the air near the ground, by the free foot and leg. This circular movement was symbolic of the moon.

After losing its religious aspect the dance merely became a charm dance (Kēlēkos Horos), using every implication of the word to fit the mood of the music and the dancers—from mere fascination to seduction. As the Byzantine Empire crumbled, the Arab and Turkish conquerors fell under the sway of its superior culture, and the Muslim overlords adopted many of its arts and were especially fascinated by this dance. Most of the dancers were Christian slave girls and the dance became a harem or odalisque dance. Eventually, this dance was performed in the bazaars and cafés simulating the court and it was primarily performed by Muslim girls; for a good dancer could have both fame and fortune and perhaps find her way to the court of the Sultan or some other wealthy nobleman.

We must not forget, though, that this dance was being performed in the countryside in a simple fashion while it was becoming an art form at the court. The girl was coquettish and her partner danced with more vigour. Frequently her actions demonstrated her domestic capabilities, but one thing remained the same and does so to this day: the girl is to move as beautifully as she can.

Characteristics: The dancers move very liltingly. The girl's movements are gentle and refined; the man is more vigorous. The girl dances for the man and tries to tell him through mime how wonderful she is. The man likewise responds, succumbs and culminates the dance by whipping out his handkerchief and embracing her with its aid, being careful not to touch the girl.

Formation: The pair face each other and circle one another.
Time: 2/4
Steps: Move to right.

1   Step on r.
2 &   Tap l. foot in front of r. and circle around to the left.
1   Set l. foot behind r.
&   Side r.
2   Cross l. foot in front of r.
&   Shift weight on to r. or point l. foot.

Move to left.

1 &   Step on l.
2 &   Tap r. foot in front of l. and circle around to the right.
1   Set r. foot behind l.
&   Side l.
2   Cross r. foot in front of l.
&   Shift weight back on to l. or point r. foot.

General movement to right.

1 &   Step on r.
2 &   Tap l. foot in front of r. and circle around to the left.
1   Set l. foot behind r.
&   Side r.
2 &   Cross l. foot in front of r.
     Repeat, etc.

Moving to right.

Steps:
1 &   Stand on r. foot, lift up l. foot bending l. knee, lifting l. foot knee high up behind, raising up and down on r. foot.
2 &   Raising up and down on r. foot, swing l. leg forward and across r. leg.
1   Step on l. foot across r.
&   Step side r.
2 &   Step on l. across r. foot.
     Repeat, moving to the left.

The steps can be minimized so that the feet keep in ground contact and the body moves up and down slightly.

Another style of the same dance which does not have the bacarollic lilt to the music is illustrated below:

Steps: I

1 & Side r.
2   Cross l. over r.
&   Bring r. slightly forward of l.
1 & Side l.
2 & Bring r. next to l.

II

1 & Forward r.
2 & Forward l. slightly ahead of r., keeping weight on r.
1 & Back on l.
2 & Bring r. back slightly in front of l., keeping weight on l.

III

1 & Forward r.
2   Slightly forward l.
&   Forward r. slightly ahead of l.
1 & Forward l.
2   Slightly forward r.
&   Forward l. slightly ahead of r.

Steps: Balance figure

1 & Side r.
2   Cross l. over r.
&   Shift weight back on r.
1 & Side l.
2   Cross r. over l.
&   Shift weight back on l.

Double cross.

1   Cross r. over l.
&   Side l.
2   Cross r. over l.
&   Circle l. foot around r.

1	Cross l. over r.
&	Side r.
2	Cross l. over r.
&	Circle r. around l.

These steps can also be performed backwards.

Move to right. (In this step the r. foot is always forward of the l.)

1	Cross r. over l., move l. to right side.
&	Move r. to right and slide l. to right side.
2	Repeat 1
&	Repeat &

(The dance is performed with the weight of the heel on the foot that is in front and on the toe of the foot that is behind.)

To change direction:

1	Cross r. over l. move l. to right side.
&	Move r. to right and slide l. to right side.
2	Cross r. over l. move l. to right side.
&	Step side right and carrying l. foot with it lightly off ground.

Now l. foot stays in front.

1	Cross l. over r., move r. to left side.
&	Move l. to left side and slide r. to left side.
2	Repeat 1
&	Repeat &

These steps can be done a number of times before changing direction. Sometimes direction is not changed.
There are many more steps, and much is left to the individual ability of the dancers: twists, turns, back bends, etc.
The hands are moved gracefully throughout the whole dance with an undulating movement of the hips.
The steps of the two styles are frequently intermingled.

ZEYBEKIKO

This dance, as its name intimates, is the dance of the Zeybeks (or Zeibeks). The name is Arabic-Persian and it means "two breeches," which is indicative of the type of short, full breeches worn by these people (similar to the Burgundian hose or full breeches worn in Western Europe during the 16th and early 17th centuries).

The Zeybeks are centered around Smyrna (Izmir) in Karamania, i.e., Western Turkey (Aegean Provinces of Turkey), and were not of Turkish or Anatolian ancestry. They are the descendants of a fusion of two peoples who founded the first city of the Zebeks in Anatolia-Tralles. One group was a Thracio-Illyrian tribe after which the city was named Tralles; the other group were Greek colonists from the Argive Peninsula.

The dance is essentially a war dance but is of a slower-moving and heavy-footed nature as compared to the Cretan Sousta. In fact, the difference between the two would be that in the Cretan Sousta, the two combatants were further apart, indicating that their weapons were javelins or long swords, etc., while in the Zeybekiko, the combatants were closer together, indicating the use of short swords or daggers, etc. In modern day usage, these differences would be likened to the movements of two boxers as opposed to the movements of two wrestlers.

Because the dancers move about and turn with their arms outstretched resembling the wings of a bird, it has been frequently called the dance of the eagle; which indeed it is when danced as a solo. The imaginary antagonist is the centre of the circle and the dancer moves as the eagle does over its prey. The eagle, since ancient times, was a symbol of power, and was identified with Zeus. The movements are also likened to a bird of prey on the attack on the ground as well as a bird's actions during the mating season and in this respect seem to parallel the shoe-plattler dances of Bavaria and Austria which symbolize the movements of chickens.

Characteristics: This dance falls into two categories, as a solo dance and as a couple dance. It runs the gamut from the slow, lazy baccarole type to that of the harsh, sharp—war-like in spirit. (A display of arms.)

Formation: The couple dance facing each other within an imaginary circle. Their various movements and turns are always done within the circle, though their form may vary, depending on whether the couple is of the opposite sex or the same. When the dance is solo, the idea of the circle is maintained with its centre gaining the importance of the opposite partner. The solo is always performed by a man.

Time: 9/8

Steps:

The variety of steps is practically endless. The patterns used depend on the mood of the dance.

Slow:	1, 2	Step l. forward.
Slow:	3, 4	Step r. side.
Slow:	5, 6	Step l. backward.
Quick:	7	Step r. backward.
Quick:	8	Cross l. over r.
Quick:	9	Step r. to side.

Variation

Slow:	1, 2	Step l. forward.
Slow:	3, 4	Step r. back diagonally, together l., step r. back. (These are three quick steps.)
Slow:	5, 6	Step l. back.
Quick:	7	Step r. side.
Quick:	8	Together l.
Quick:	9	Step r. side.

Slow:	1, 2	Step l. forward.
Slow:	3, 4	Cross r. behind l.
Slow:	5, 6	Cross l. behind r.

Quick: 7   Side r.
Quick: 8   Cross l. over r.
Quick: 9   Side r.

Slow: 1, 2   Cross l. over r.
Slow: 3, 4   Cross r. over l. and side l. to left.
Slow: 5, 6   Cross r. over l.
Quick: 7   Cross l. foot over r. by swinging it in an arc.
Quick: 8   Continue turning to right by stepping r.
Quick: 9   Continue turning to right by stepping on l. facing partner again.

ILLUSTRATIVE FOOT PATTERNS
OF THE DANCES

These foot patterns serve only as a general guide not to be strictly adhered to.

(see following pages)

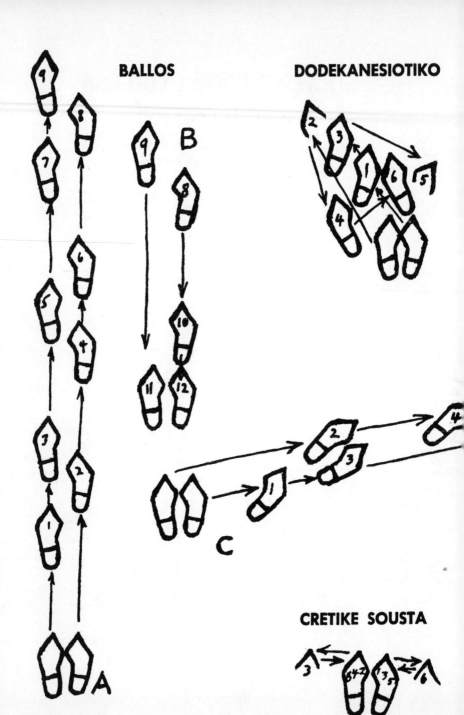

BALLOS

DODEKANESIOTIKO

CRETIKE SOUSTA

HASSAPIKO

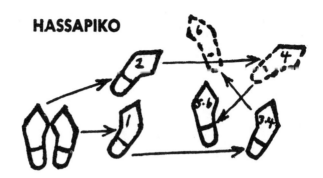

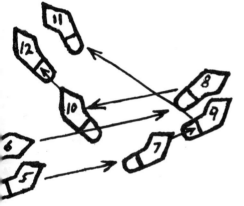

VARI HASSAPIKO

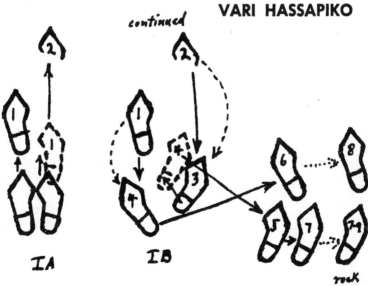

continued

IA

IB

rock

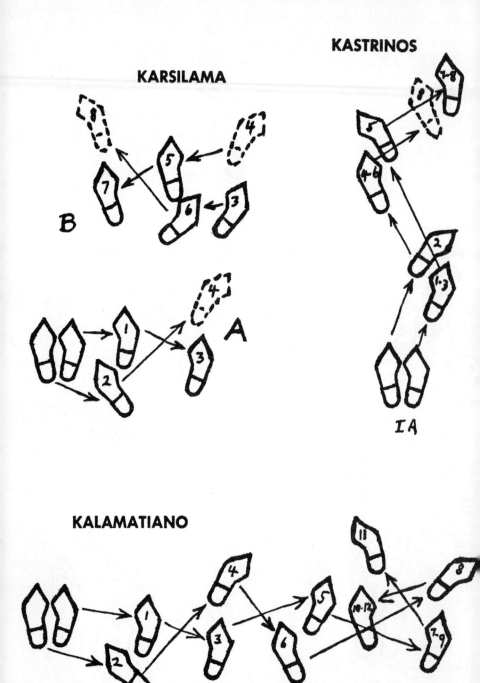

KASTRINOS

KARSILAMA

B

A

IA

KALAMATIANO

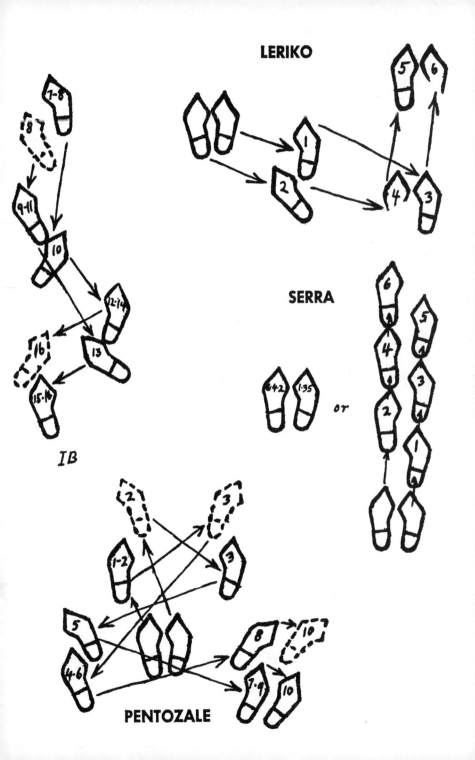

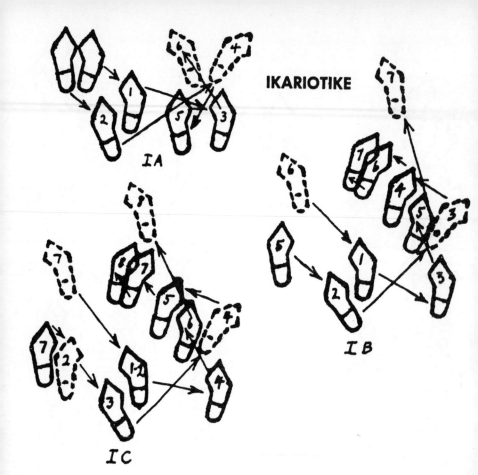

IKARIOTIKE

IA

IB

IC

KARPATHIRE

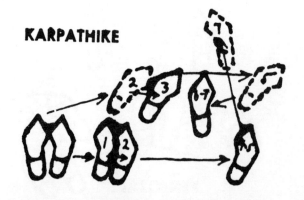

KASSIOTIKE SOUSTA

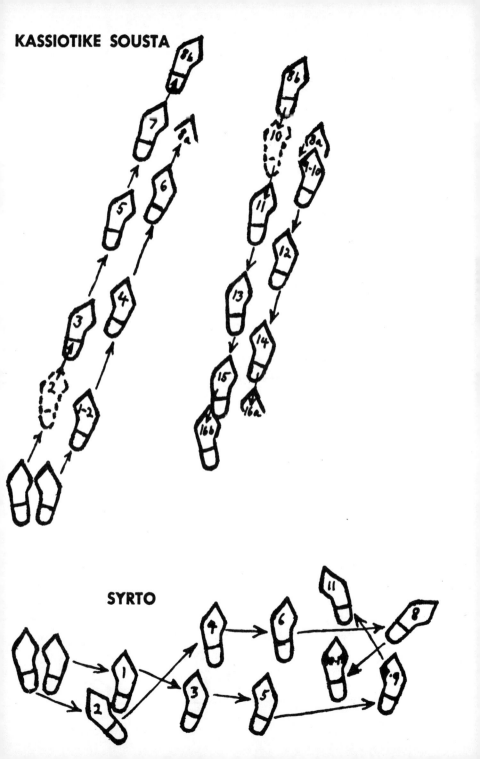

SYRTO

RODITIOUN SOUSTA (A)

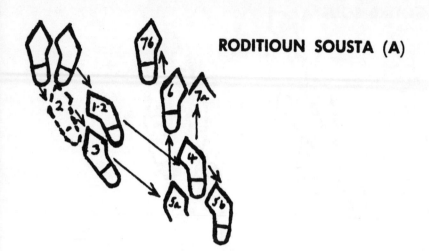

RODITIOUN SOUSTA (B)

CRETIKE SYRTO

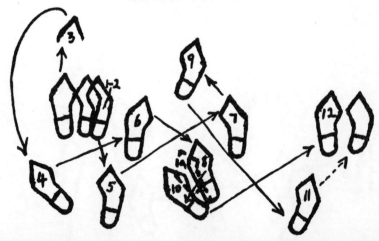

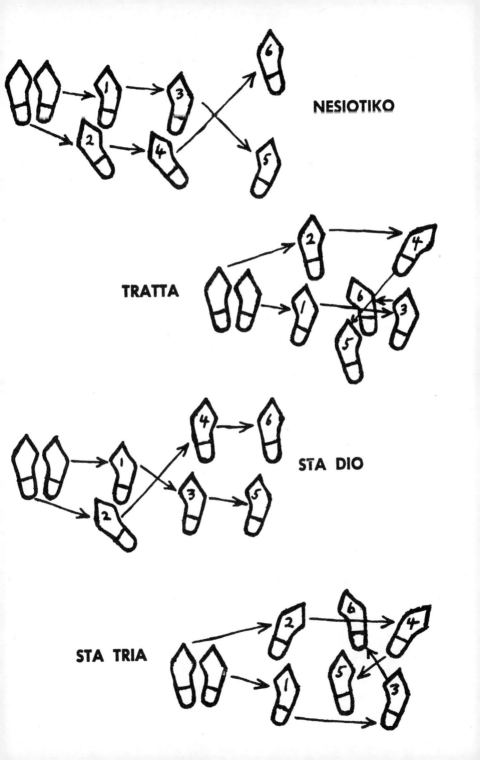

NESIOTIKO

TRATTA

STA DIO

STA TRIA

TIK

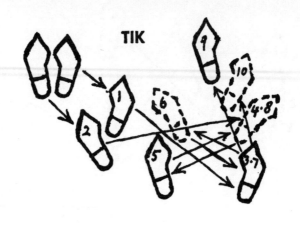

TSAMIKO

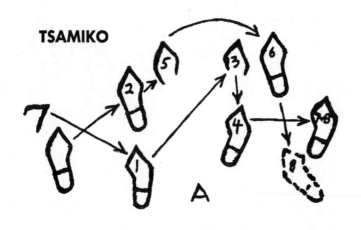

A

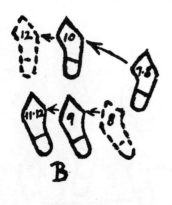

B

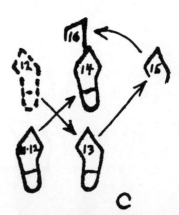

C

TSIFTE TELLI

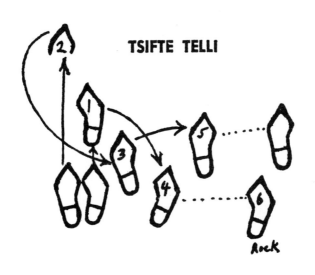

Rock

ZEYBEKIKO

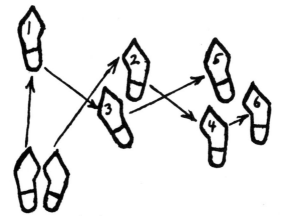

GLOSSARY

Bállos (*It.*), dance.
Çífte Télli (*Turk.*), two strings.
Crētiké Soústa (*Gr.*), from the Island of Crete.
Crētikó Syrtó (*Gr.*), from the Island of Crete.
Dodékanēsiótiko (*Gr.*), from the Twelve Islands.
Dodékanēsiótikē Soústa (*Gr.*), from the Twelve Islands.
Hassápiko (*Turk.*), butcher.
Ikariótiko (*Gr.*), from Ikaria Island.
Kalamatianó (*Gr.*), from Kalamata.
Karpáthiko (*Gr.*), from Karpathos Island.
Karşilamás (*Turk.*), face to face.
Kassiótikē (*Gr.*), from Kassos Island.
Kastrinós (*Gr.*), from Kastron; (*It.*), fort.
Kēlikós (*Gr.*), charm dance.
Lerikó (*Gr.*), from Leros Island.
Mahéra (*Gr.*), sword dance.
Nēsiótiko (*Gr.*), from an island.
Pēdēchtó (*Gr.*), jumping dance.
Pentozálēs (*Gr.*), a five-step pattern.
Pyrrhichó (*Gr.*), war dance.
Rodítioun (*Gr.*), of Rhodes.
Sérra (*Gr.*), from the Serra River region.
Sta Dío (*Gr.*), two steps.
Sta Tría (*Gr.*), three steps.
Syrtós (*Gr.*), drag.
Tik (*Turk.*), upright.
Trátta (*Gr.*), fishing net.
Tsámiko (*Gr.*), from the Çams.
Varí Hassápiko (*Gr.*), Heavy Hassapiko.
Zeybékiko (*Gr.*), from the Zeybeks.